A Keepsake to Treasure

There is no lovelier gift to your child than a personal letter written upon the occasion of his or her birth to be shared at a time in the distant future. Here is the place to share your thoughts, hopes and dreams for the future...a place to tell your baby who you are...a place to remember your pregnancy and delivery...and a place to note anything you wish your child to know.

CHILD'S NAME

DATE OF BIRTH

PLACE OF BIRTH

MOTHER   AGE

FATHER   AGE

CURRENT ADDRESS

MATERNAL GRANDMOTHER

MATERNAL GRANDFATHER

PATERNAL GRANDMOTHER

PATERNAL GRANDFATHER

(STEP) GRANDPARENT

(STEP) GRANDPARENT

Attach baby photo here

Date

To my dearest little one,

from

The greatest gifts you can give your children
are roots and wings.

There is no flower in the world that breathes
a sweeter fragrance than a
freshly bathed baby.

A baby is a glimpse of heaven—especially
when asleep.

Sleep is something that science cannot abolish
but babies can.

Every new baby brings the message that the
world should continue.

When your baby looks into your eyes
and you know it's yours,
it changes you forever.

Babies are as much an instrument of nourishment
for us as we are for them.

A baby is fed with milk and praise.

Who else but a baby could totally captivate an
audience by being watched
while sleeping.

A baby is a reason to celebrate the universe.

A baby is a gift wrapped in love and tied up
with heartstrings.

A baby teaches you many things, including
how much patience you have.

Parenthood is a job where the overtime is an unpaid benefit.

There are no magic answers in raising
children—only magic moments.

A parent's love is not blind.
It's just very nearsighted.

The best part of having a baby is seeing the
world anew—trees, flowers,
animals and all.

A baby will sleep calmly until the moment
you sit down to dinner.

Nothing else will ever make us as happy or
sad, as proud or tired, as a
child.

A baby sells itself without needing to advertise.

Our children are extensions of ourselves
in ways our parents are not, nor our brothers,
sisters or spouses.

A baby will make loving stronger,
your days shorter, your nights longer,
your home happier, your clothes shabbier,
the past forgotten and the future a
wonder worth waiting for.

Design, Production & Printing by
Pettit Network, Afton MN

Book Peddlers
15245 Minnetonka Blvd, Minnetonka, MN 55345
phone 952-912-0036 • fax 952-912-0105
www.bookpeddlers.com
book trade distributor: PGW

To order more copies
or for a copy of our catalog
call 1-800-255-3379.

Printed in
Hong Kong

01 02 03 04 05 06 07 08   09 10 9 8 7 6 5 4 3 2 1